Learn to Read
Literacy Series | Book 1

Letter Names
and Sounds

STARTUP
LEARNING

Startup Learning, PBC
A public benefit corporation
www.LearnToReadOnline.org
info@LearnToReadOnline.org

ISBN 978-1-942696-11-7

Welcome to Learn to Read!

The **Learn to Read Letter Names and Sounds Workbook** addresses the important concepts of letter names and consonant sounds. The "Imaginary Picture Story" introduces students to consonant sounds in a dynamic narrative. While engaged in the story, students will associate the letters with images, leading to long-term memorization of the letter names and sounds.

New! Access recorded video teaching sessions for each book lesson.

We recommend that you **register** as a user of the book at the **Learn to Read Online** website: LearnToReadOnline.org.

There you can access a **Learning Management System** that provides a teaching session for each page in this book. (Note: you may preview several **free** teaching sessions for each Learn to Read book at the website: LearnToReadOnline.org/all-courses.)

When you select any of the listed courses you will see all the sessions that are available, with a monthly subscription. Once you complete registration you will receive a coupon giving you a discounted price for the teaching sessions in this book.

We are pleased to have the opportunity to provide your child with a rewarding experience for academic success in the foundational skills of learning to read!

Sincerely,

Vivian Mendoza
Director, Literacy Curriculum

Learn to Read books in this series

Book 1: Letter Names and Sounds   Book 5: Digraphs and Blends

Book 2: Long Vowels   Book 6: Two-Syllable Words

Book 3: Short Vowels   Book 7: Introduction to Vowel Teams

Book 4: Long and Short Vowels   Book 8: Expanded Vowel Teams

Table of Contents

Contributors to the Workbook

Vivian Mendoza

Donna Davies

Donna Davies
Illustrator

Bill Haff
Graphic Design

Ben Kuyper
Cover Design

Letter Names

CCSS.ELALITERACY.RF.K.1D

Teachers: Have students point to each letter and say its name.

Aa Bb Cc

Dd Ee Ff

Gg Hh Ii

Jj Kk Ll

Mm Nn Oo

Pp Qq Rr

Ss Tt Uu

Vv Ww Xx

Yy Zz

Letter Sounds

CCSS.ELALITERACY.RF.K.3.A

Teachers: Have students point to each consonant and say its sound.

	/b^uh/	/k^h/
a*	b	c*

/d^uh/		/f^ff/
d	e*	f

/g^uh/	/h^uh/	
g*	h	i*

/j^uh/	/k^h/	/L^LL/
j	k	l

/m^mm/	/n^nn/	
m	n	o*

/p^uh/	/kw^uh/	/r^rr/
p	q	r

/s^ss/	/t^uh/	
s*	t	u*

/v^vv/	/w^uh/	/ks^ss/
v	w	x

/y^uh/	/z^zz/	
y*	z	**✶** indicates letters that make more than one sound

Vowels and the Reading Code

Teachers: Have students point to each vowel and say the Reading Code. Go down the Long Vowel column first, then move to the Short Vowels.

Long Vowels	**Short Vowels**

a-with-a-vowel-after
says:

ā

acorn

a-without-a-vowel-after
says:

ă

apple

e-with-a-vowel-after
says:

ē

eagle

e-without-a-vowel-after
says:

ĕ

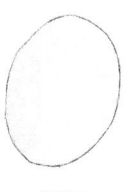
egg

i-with-a-vowel-after
says:

ī

ice cream

i-without-a-vowel-after
says:

ĭ

igloo

o-with-a-vowel-after
says:

ō

oboe

o-without-a-vowel-after
says:

ŏ

ox

u-with-a-vowel-after
says:

ū

unicorn

u-without-a-vowel-after
says:

ŭ

Learning to Read
Letter Names and Sounds

Lesson 1

STARTUP
LEARNING

The recorded teaching sessions
for this lesson can be accessed
at LearnToReadOnline.org.

Prince Peter and Princess Pam

The Sounds of All the Letters

STARTUP
LEARNING

The Sounds of the Letters | Letters "Aa" to "Ii"   CCSS.ELA-LITERACY.RF.K.3.A

Once upon a time, there lived two children,
Princess Pam and Prince Peter,
who were very adventurous.

The Sounds of the Letters | Letters "Aa" to "Ii"   CCSS.ELA-LITERACY.RF.K.3.A

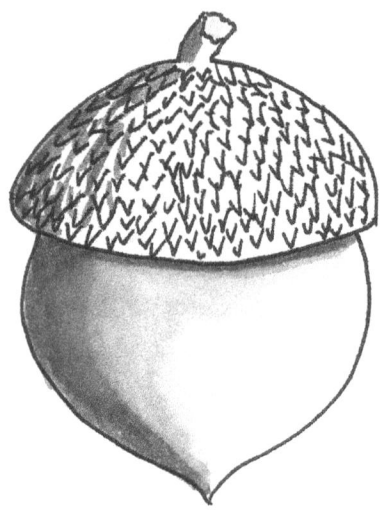

*They loved to collect **acorns**
in the woods and eat **apples**
from the orchard.*

The Sounds of the Letters | Letters "Aa" to "Ii"   CCSS.ELA-LITERACY.RF.K.3.A

*One time while they were playing in the woods, they bumped into the back of a baby **bear**!*

The Sounds of the Letters | Letters "Aa" to "Ii"   CCSS.ELA-LITERACY.RF.K.3.A

*They were so surprised, they ran all the way back to their home in the **castle**.*

The Sounds of the Letters | Letters "Aa" to "Ii"

CCSS.ELA-LITERACY.RF.K.3.A

Dd

*At home, they pet their **dog** on her head so she lifted her tail straight up and wagged it happily.*

The Sounds of the Letters | Letters "Aa" to "Ii"　　CCSS.ELA-LITERACY.RF.K.3.A

Ee

*Overhead, they saw an **eagle** soar and drop an **egg** he had taken from a nest.*

The Sounds of the Letters | Letters "Aa" to "Ii"   CCSS.ELA-LITERACY.RF.K.3.A

Ff

*When they skipped over the old stone bridge, they saw a **fish** jump out of the water.*

The Sounds of the Letters | Letters "Aa" to "Ii"   CCSS.ELA-LITERACY.RF.K.3.A

Gg

Then the curious children
*opened a garden **gate**,*

The Sounds of the Letters | Letters "Aa" to "Ii"

CCSS.ELA-LITERACY.RF.K.3.A

Hh

*Inside was a huge **hive**
built for bees.*

The Sounds of the Letters | Letters "Aa" to "Ii"   CCSS.ELA-LITERACY.RF.K.3.A

The beekeeper gave them
ice cream cones.

That made them shiver so they imagined
they were living in an ***igloo***.

The Sounds of the Letters | Letters "Aa" to "Ii"   CCSS.ELA-LITERACY.RF.K.3.A

Beginning Sounds

Directions: Circle the letter that makes the beginning SOUND for each drawing. The letters on this page are in the "a" to "i" range.

Example:

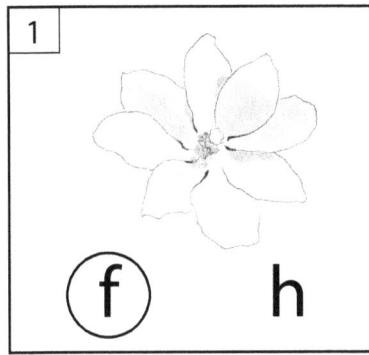

1   (f)   h

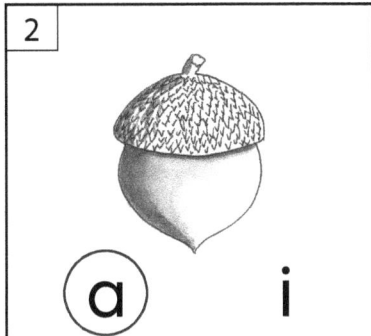

2   (a)   i

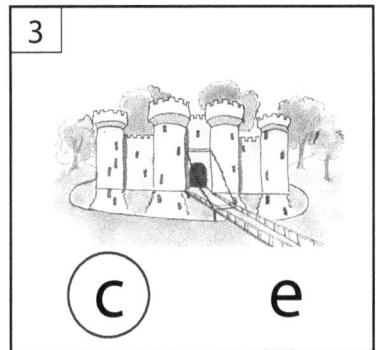

3   (c)   e

4   a   (e)

5   f   (d)

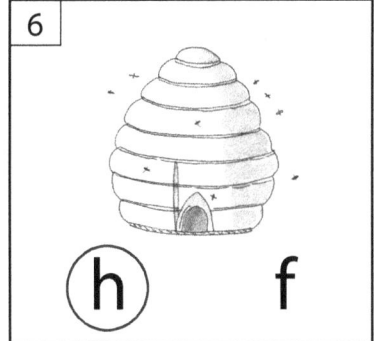

6   (h)   f

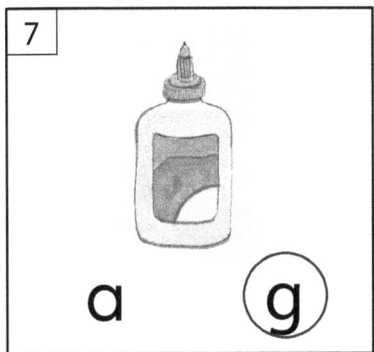

7   a   (g)

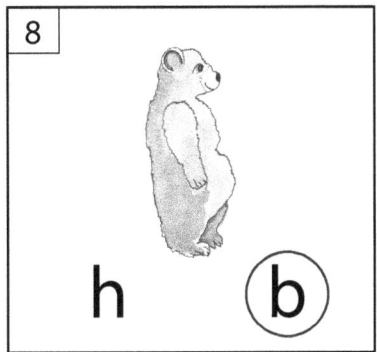

8   h   (b)

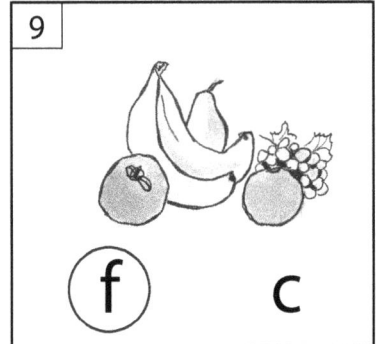

9   (f)   c

1. flower 2. acorn 3. castle 4. eagle 5. dog 6. hive 7. glue 8. bear 9. fruit

The Sounds of the Letters | Letters "Aa" to "Ii"

CCSS.ELA-LITERACY.RF.K.3.A

Beginning Sounds

Directions: Circle the letter that makes the beginning SOUND for each drawing. The letters on this page are in the "a" to "i" range.

Example:

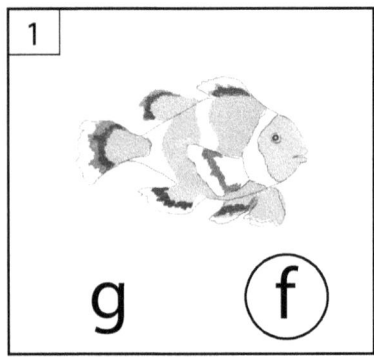

1

g   (f)

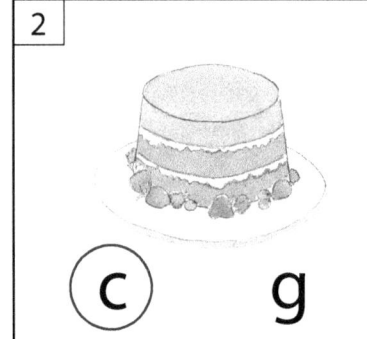

2

(c)   g

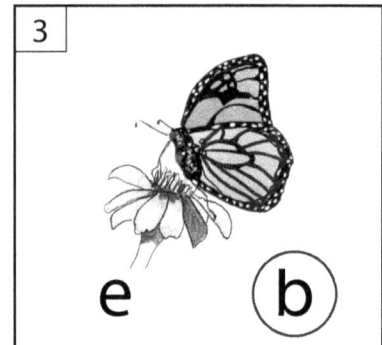

3

e   (b)

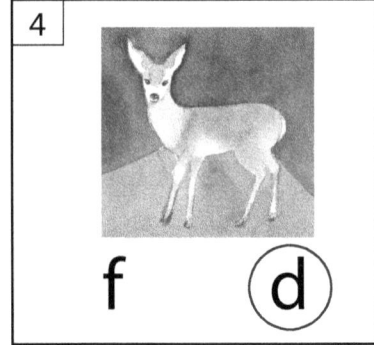

4

f   (d)

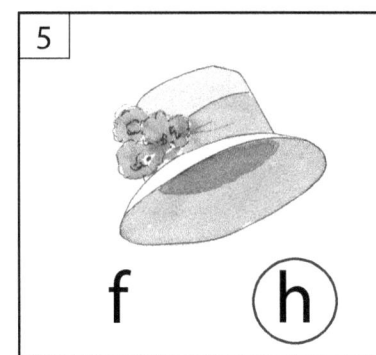

5

f   (h)

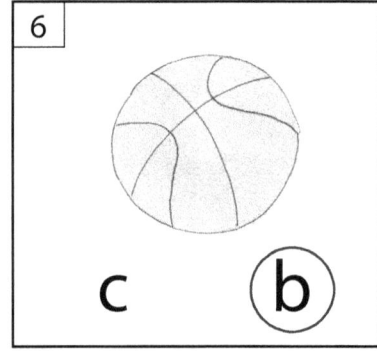

6

c   (b)

7

(d)   a

8

(i)   a

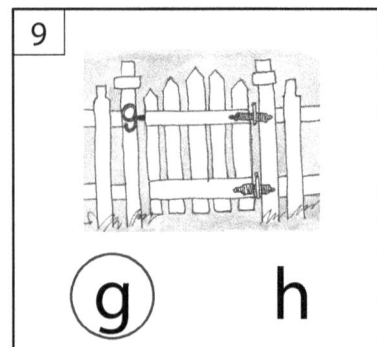

9

(g)   h

1. fish 2. cake 3. butterfly 4. deer 5. hat 6. ball 7. duck 8. ice cream 9. gate

The Names of the Letters | Letters "Aa" to "Ii"

Upper and Lowercase Letter Names

Directions: Look at the uppercase letters in each balloon. Circle the matching upper and lowercase letters in the box. Then in each balloon draw a line from the uppercase letter to the lowercase letter with the same name.

A B C D E F G H I J K L M N O P Q R S T U V W X Y Z
a b c d e f g h i j k l m n o p q r s t u v w x y z

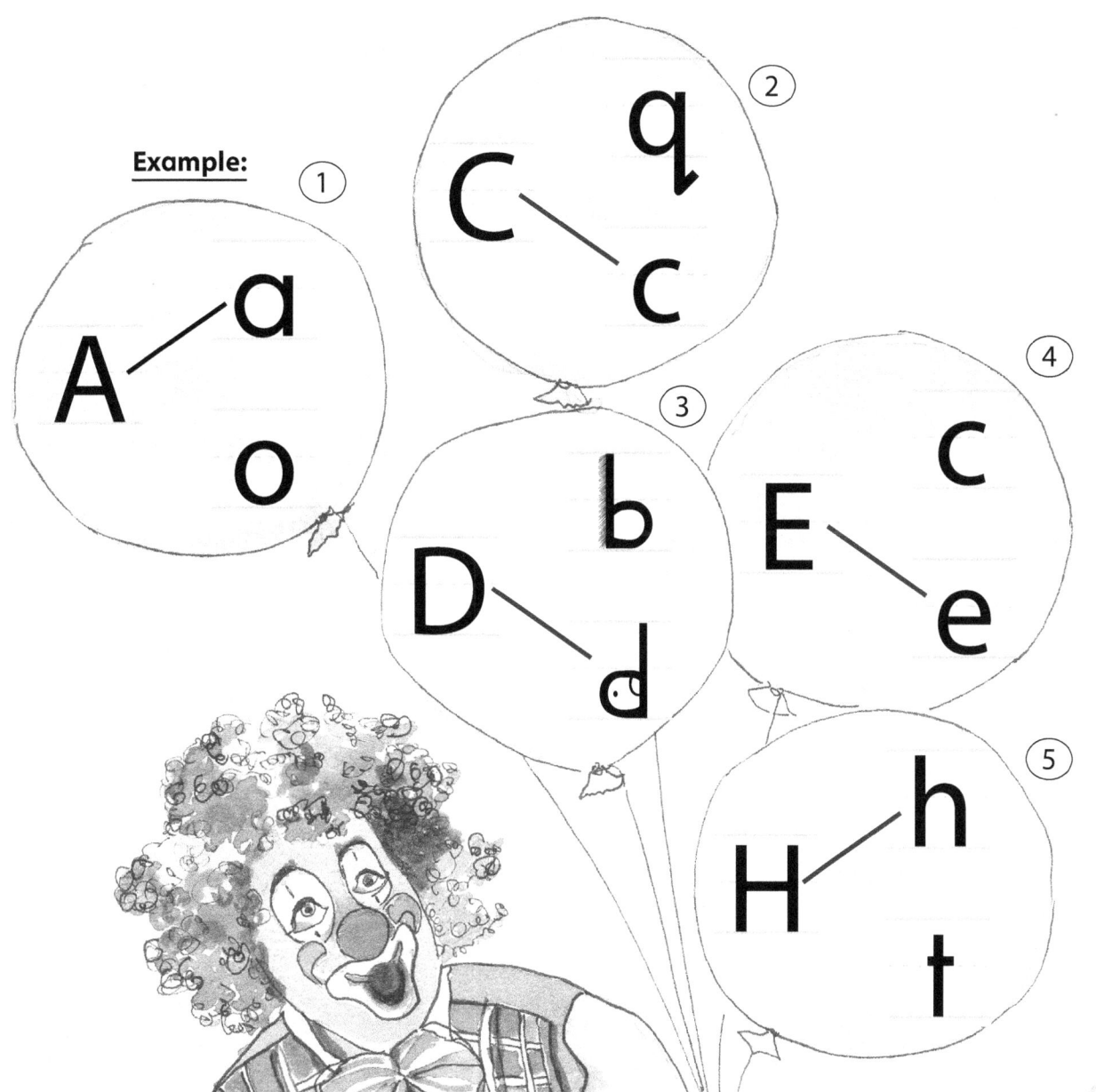

Example:
① A — a o

② C — q c

③ D — b d

④ E c — e

⑤ H — h t

The Names of the Letters | Letters "Aa" to "Ii"

Upper and Lowercase Letter Names

Directions: Look at the uppercase letters in each balloon. Circle the matching upper and lowercase letters in the box. Then in each balloon draw a line from the uppercase letter to the lowercase letter with the same name.

A B C D E F G H I J K L M N O P Q R S T U V W X Y Z
a b c d e f g h i j k l m n o p q r s t u v w x y z

Example:

The Names of the Letters | Letters "Aa" to "Ii"

Matching Upper and Lowercase Letters

Directions: Draw a line from the uppercase letter in the left column to the matching lowercase letter in the right column.

A B C D E F G H I J K L M N O P Q R S T U V W X Y Z
a b c d e f g h i j k l m n o p q r s t u v w x y z

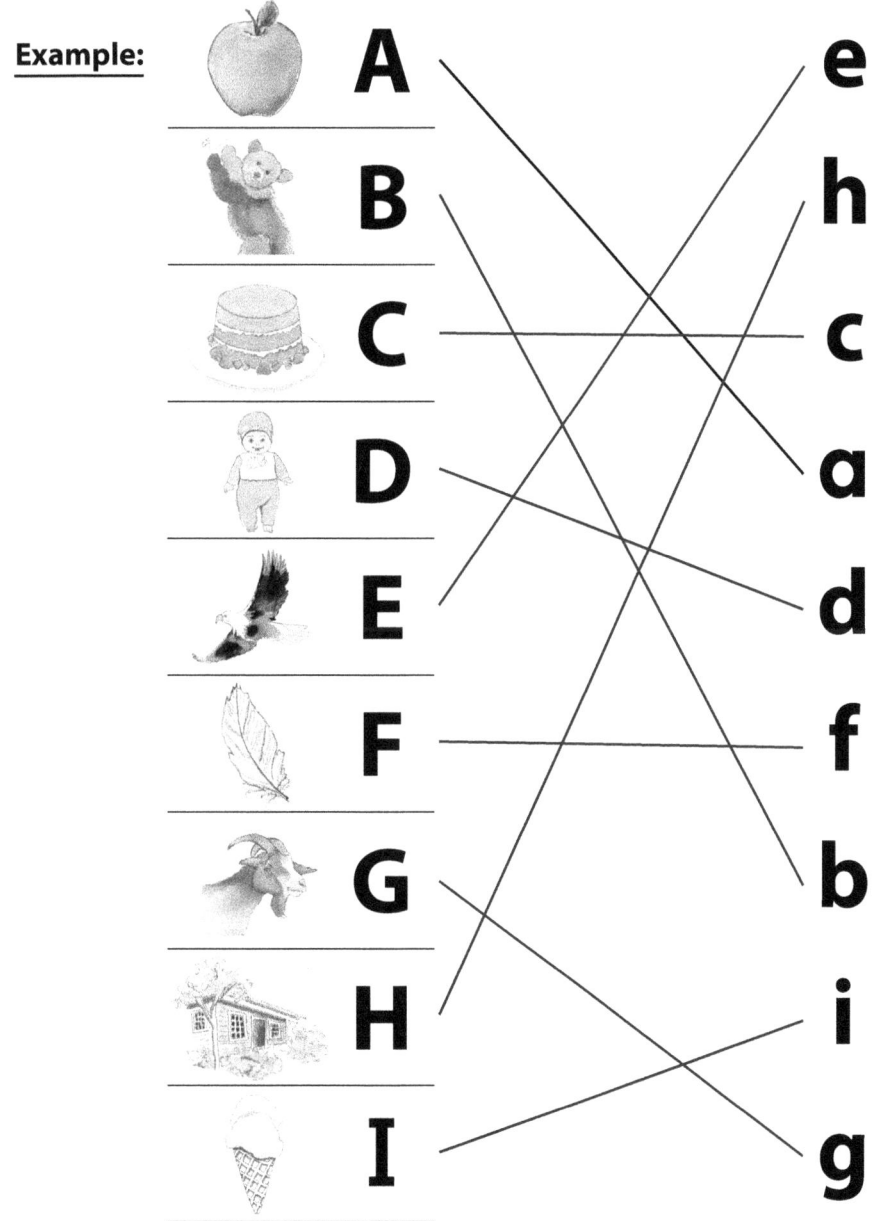

Example:

A
B
C
D
E
F
G
H
I

e
h
c
a
d
f
b
i
g

The Names of the Letters | Letters "Aa" to "Ii"

Matching Upper and Lowercase Letters

<u>**Directions:**</u> Cut and paste the lowercase letters next to the correct capital letters.

A B C D E F G H I J K L M N O P Q R S T U V W X Y Z
a b c d e f g h i j k l m n o p q r s t u v w x y z

Example:

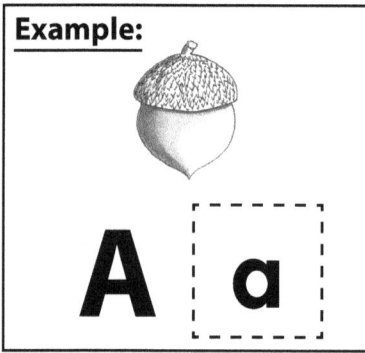

A | a |

B | b |

C | c |

D | d |

E | e |

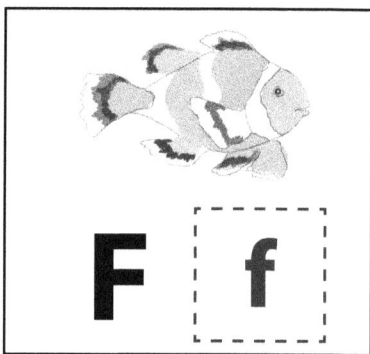

F | f |

G | g |

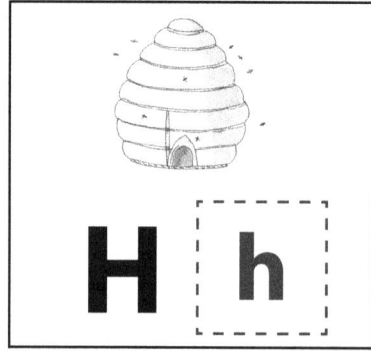

H | h |

I | i |

a e h c d f b i g

Learning to Read
Letter Names and Sounds
Lesson 2

STARTUP
LEARNING

The recorded teaching sessions
for this lesson can be accessed
at LearnToReadOnline.org.

The Sounds of the Letters | Letters "Jj" to "Rr"

In the last lesson, Princess Pam and Prince Peter ate ice cream cones, that made them shiver like they were living in an igloo! Let's find out what happens next!

Jj

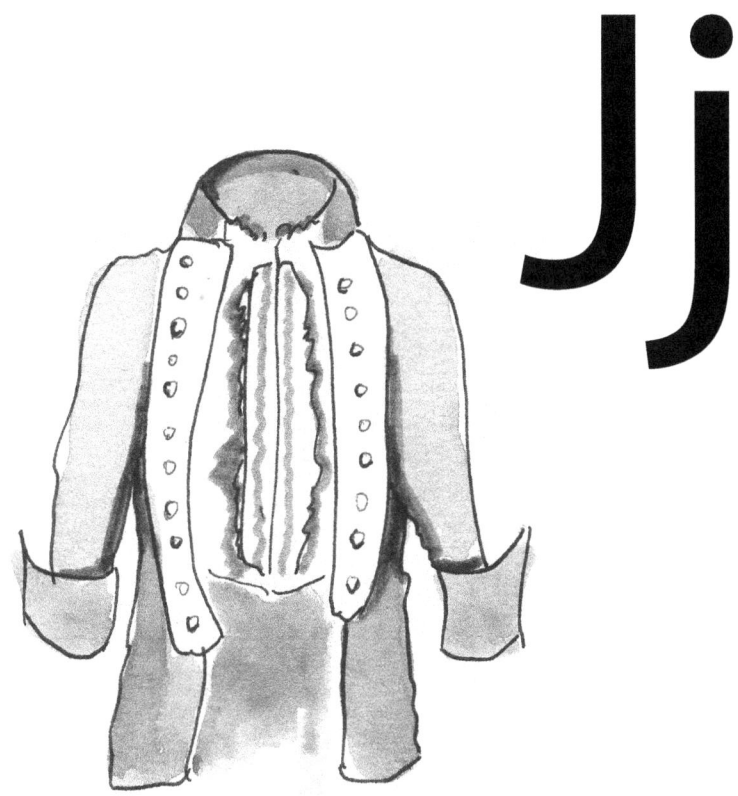

*Prince Peter quickly put on his **jacket** to keep warm.*

The Sounds of the Letters | Letters "Jj" to "Rr"

CCSS.ELA-LITERACY.RF.K.3.A

Kk

*Then, their father, **King Kenneth**, joined them in the garden.*

The Sounds of the Letters | Letters "Jj" to "Rr"

CCSS.ELA-LITERACY.RF.K.3.A

Ll

*He helped them collect lovely fall **leaves**.*

Mm

*A tiny **mouse** scurried out
from under a pile of leaves.*

Nn

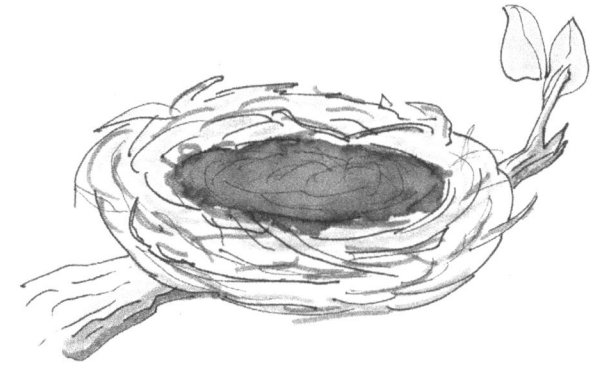

*Then Princess Pam noticed
a neatly built **nest** in a tree.*

The Sounds of the Letters | Letters "Jj" to "Rr"   CCSS.ELA-LITERACY.RF.K.3.A

*Nearby, their friend Olivia
played music on an **oboe**.
She sat on a cart pulled by an **ox**.*

The Sounds of the Letters | Letters "Jj" to "Rr"

CCSS.ELA-LITERACY.RF.K.3.A

Pp

*Olivia gave them a pretty **pumpkin** from her garden.*

They showed it to their mother,
Queen Quinn*, who was*
making a quilt.

The Sounds of the Letters | Letters "Jj" to "Rr"   CCSS.ELA-LITERACY.RF.K.3.A

Rr

*Then, King Kenneth gave the queen a beautiful red **rose**.*

The Sounds of the Letters | Letters "Jj" to "Rr"   CCSS.ELA-LITERACY.RF.K.3.A

Beginning Sounds

Directions: Circle the letter that makes the beginning SOUND for each drawing. The letters on this page are in the "j" to "r" range.

Example:

1. (k)   m

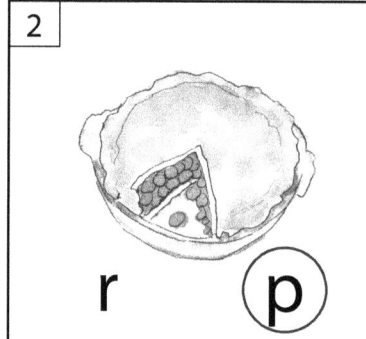
2. r   (p)

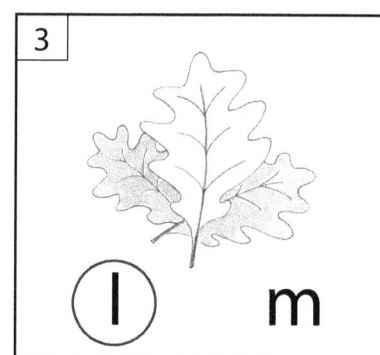
3. (l)   m

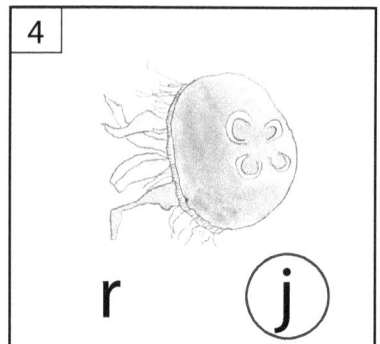
4. r   (j)

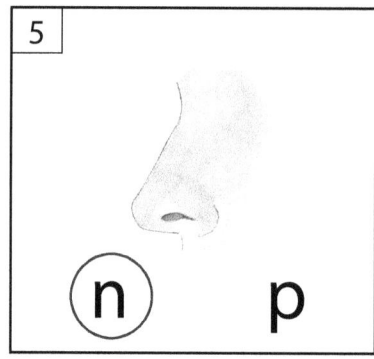
5. (n)   p

6. n   (r)

7. (k)   n

8. q   (m)

9. l   (r)

1. kitten 2. pie 3. leaves 4. jellyfish 5. nose 6. rain 7. king 8. moon 9. rose

The Sounds of the Letters | Letters "Jj" to "Rr"   CCSS.ELA-LITERACY.RF.K.3.A

Beginning Sounds

Directions: Circle the letter that makes the beginning SOUND for each drawing. The letters on this page are in the "j" to "r" range.

Example:

1  (l̃) n	**2**  n (q̃)	**3** 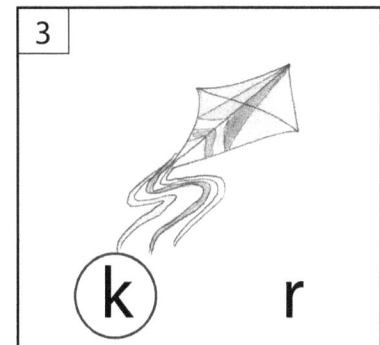 (k̃) r
4 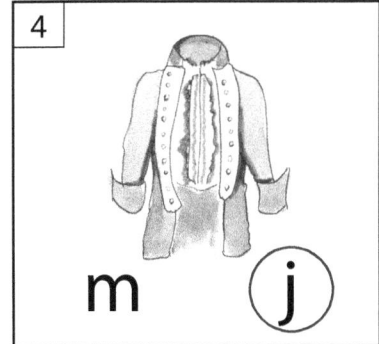 m (j̃)	**5** 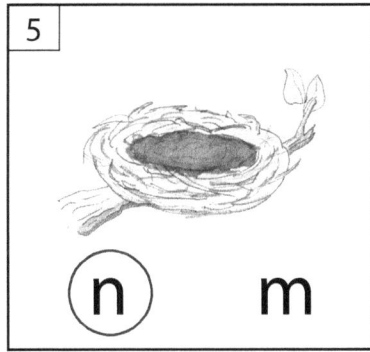 (ñ) m	**6** 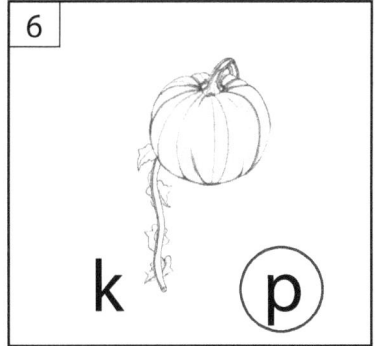 k (p̃)
7 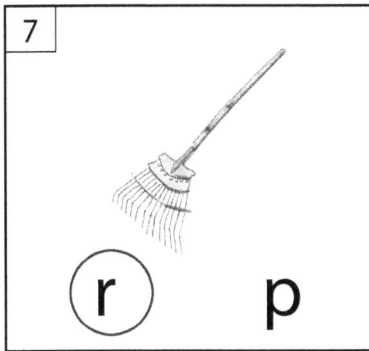 (r̃) p	**8** 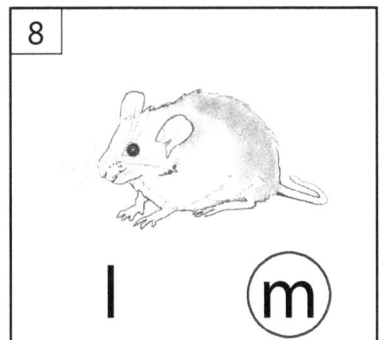 l (m̃)	**9** 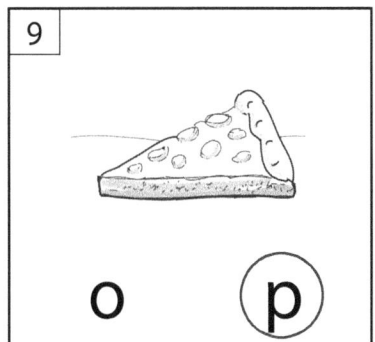 o (p̃)

1. lion 2. queen 3. kite 4. jacket 5. nest 6. pumpkin 7. rake 8. mouse 9. pizza

The Names of the Letters | Letters "Jj" to "Rr"

Upper and Lowercase Letter Names

Directions: Look at the uppercase letters in each balloon. Circle the matching upper and lowercase letters in the box. Then in each balloon draw a line from the uppercase letter to the lowercase letter with the same name.

A B C D E F G H I J K L M N O P Q R S T U V W X Y Z
a b c d e f g h i j k l m n o p q r s t u v w x y z

Example:

The Names of the Letters | Letters "Jj" to "Rr"

Matching Upper and Lowercase Letters

Directions: Draw a line from the uppercase letter in the left column to the matching lowercase letter in the right column.

A B C D E F G H I J K L M N O P Q R S T U V W X Y Z
a b c d e f g h i j k l m n o p q r s t u v w x y z

Example:

The Names of the Letters | Letters "Jj" to "Rr"

Matching Upper and Lowercase Letters

Directions: Cut and paste the lowercase letters next to the correct capital letters.

A B C D E F G H I J K L M N O P Q R S T U V W X Y Z
a b c d e f g h i j k l m n o p q r s t u v w x y z

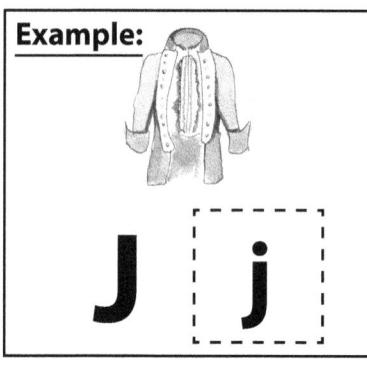

Example:

J j

K k

L l

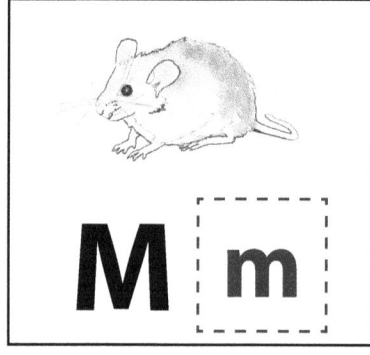

M m

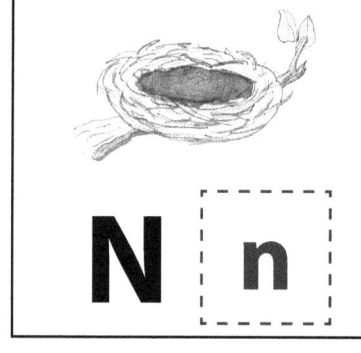

N n

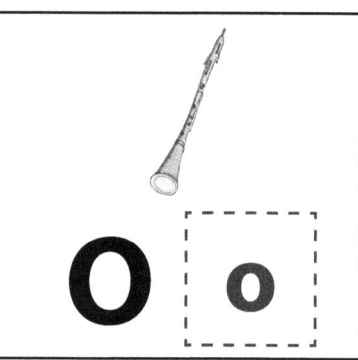

O o

P p

Q q

R r

k m l j r q o n p

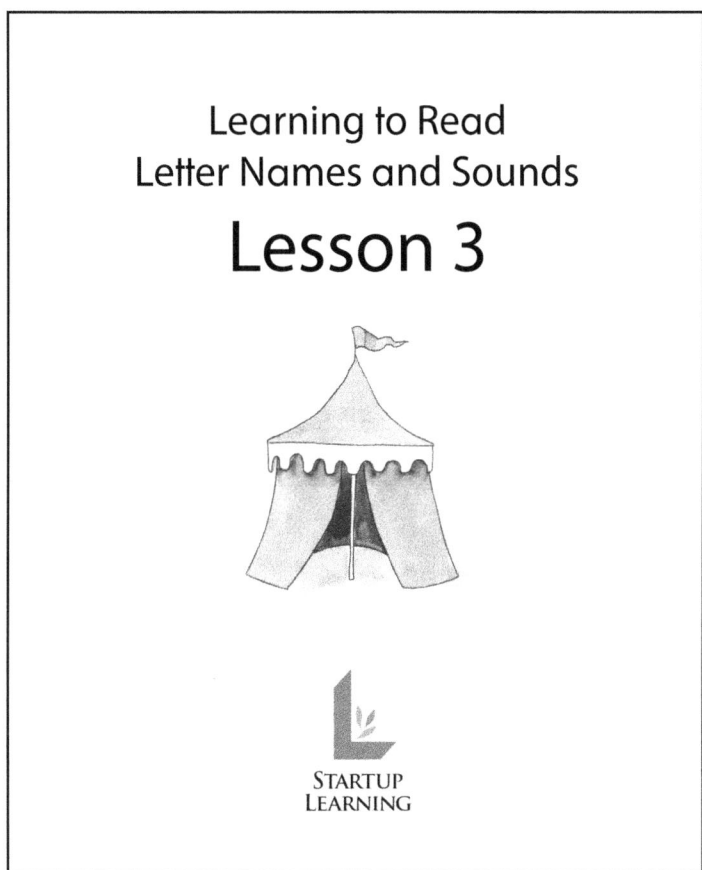

Learning to Read
Letter Names and Sounds

Lesson 3

STARTUP
LEARNING

The recorded teaching sessions
for this lesson can be accessed
at LearnToReadOnline.org.

The Sounds of the Letters | Letters "Ss" to "Zz"

In the last lesson, King Kenneth gave the queen a beautiful red rose. Let's keep reading to find out what happens next!

_____

The Sounds of the Letters | Letters "Ss" to "Zz"   CCSS.ELA-LITERACY.RF.K.3.A

*The next day in the woods,
the children saw a **snake**
slither under a rock.*

The Sounds of the Letters | Letters "Ss" to "Zz"   CCSS.ELA-LITERACY.RF.K.3.A

T t

*As they entered the town,
they saw the circus **tent** going up.*

The Sounds of the Letters | Letters "Ss" to "Zz"

CCSS.ELA-LITERACY.RF.K.3.A

*They pretended to be **unicorns**.*
But rain began to fall
*so they opened their **umbrella**.*

The Sounds of the Letters | Letters "Ss" to "Zz"   CCSS.ELA-LITERACY.RF.K.3.A

Vv

*While speeding home in the rain, Prince Peter tripped on a **vine**, fell over, and bent their umbrella.*

The Sounds of the Letters | Letters "Ss" to "Zz"   CCSS.ELA-LITERACY.RF.K.3.A

Ww

*But they kept running on a trail that went right past a wonderful **waterfall**.*

The Sounds of the Letters | Letters "Ss" to "Zz"

CCSS.ELA-LITERACY.RF.K.3.A

fix

Xx

*Back in the castle, Prince Peter tried to **fix** their bent umbrella.*

The Sounds of the Letters | Letters "Ss" to "Zz"

CCSS.ELA-LITERACY.RF.K.3.A

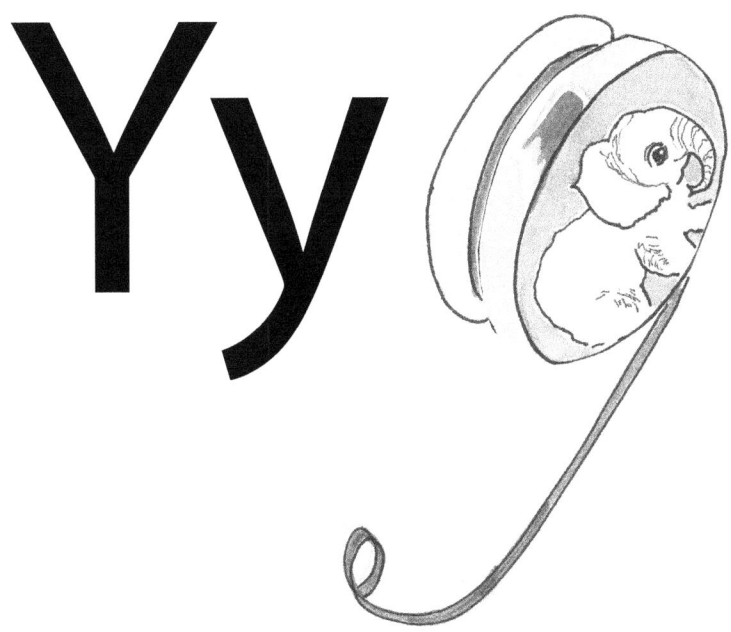

*Meanwhile, Princess Pam
played with her **yo-yo**.*

The Sounds of the Letters | Letters "Ss" to "Zz"   CCSS.ELA-LITERACY.RF.K.3.A

Zz

The elephant on it reminded her
*they would soon see a **zebra***
in a traveling circus.

The Sounds of the Letters | Letters "Ss" to "Zz"

CCSS.ELA-LITERACY.RF.K.3.A

Beginning Sounds

Directions: Circle the letter that makes the beginning SOUND for each drawing. The letters on this page are in the "s" to "z" range.

Example:

1 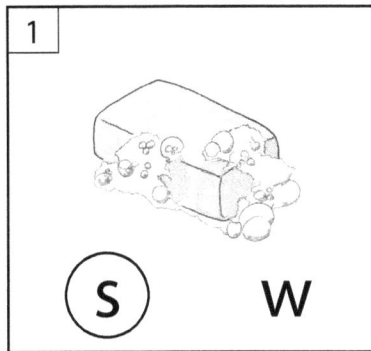 (s) w	2 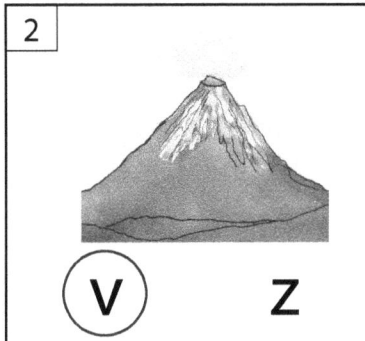 (v) z	3 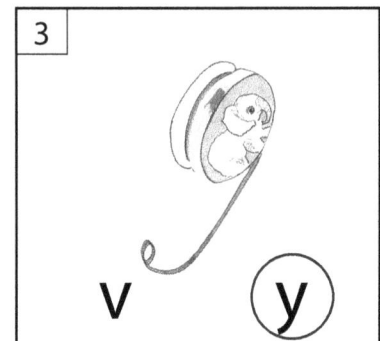 v (y)
4 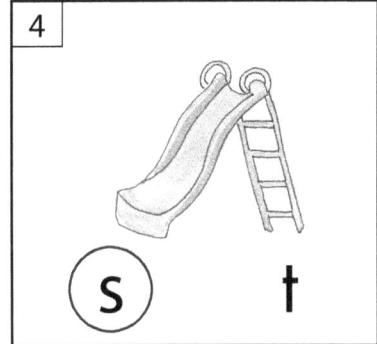 (s) t	5 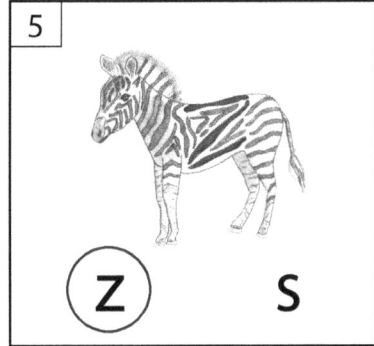 (z) s	6 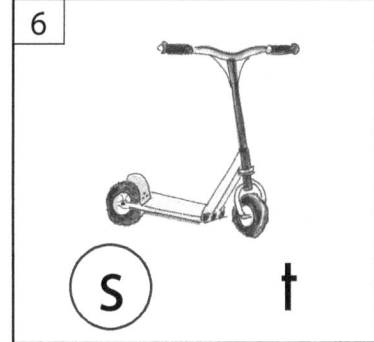 (s) t
7 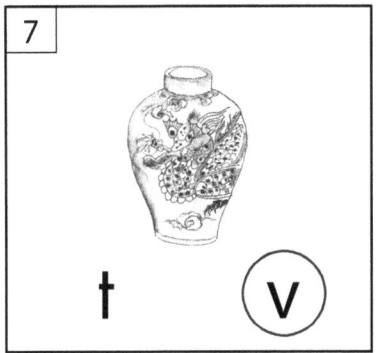 t (v)	8  u (w)	9 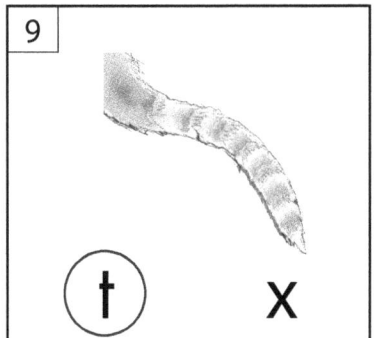 (t) x

1. soap 2. volcano 3. yo-yo 4. slide 5. zebra 6. scooter 7. vase 8. waterfall 9. tail

The Sounds of the Letters | Letters "Ss" to "Zz"   CCSS.ELA-LITERACY.RF.K.3.A

Beginning Sounds

Directions: Circle the letter that makes the beginning SOUND for each drawing. The letters on this page are in the "s" to "z" range.

Example:

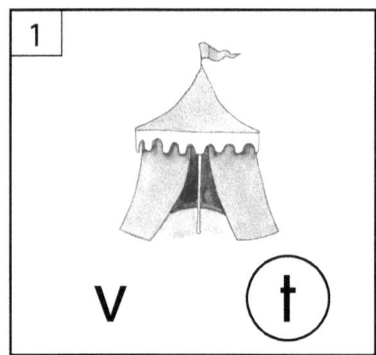

1
v   (t)

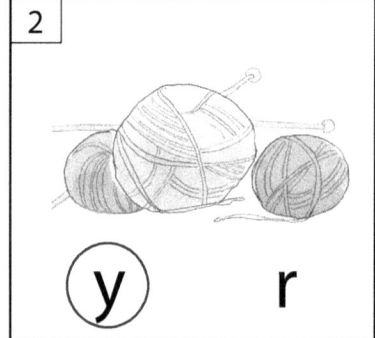

2
(y)   r

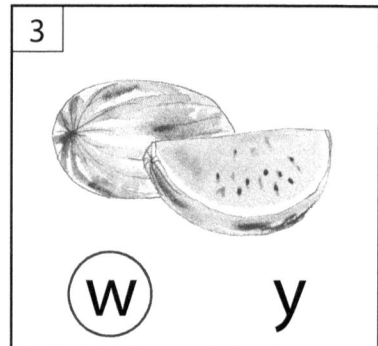

3
(w)   y

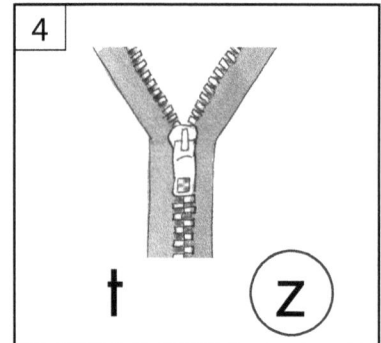

4
t   (z)

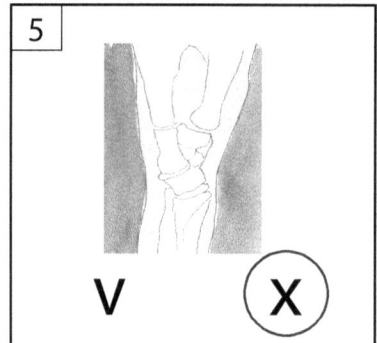

5
v   (x)

6
(s)   z

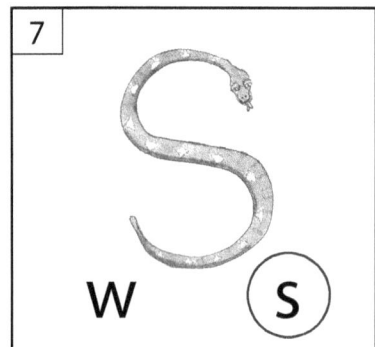

7
w   (s)

8
x   (t)

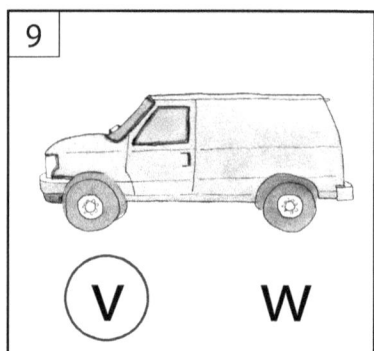

9
(v)   w

1. tent 2. yarn 3. watermelon 4. zipper 5. x-ray 6. sun 7. snake 8. turtle 9. van

The Names of the Letters | Letters "Ss" to "Zz"

Upper and Lowercase Letter Names

Directions: Look at the uppercase letters in each balloon. Circle the matching upper and lowercase letters in the box. Then in each balloon draw a line from the uppercase letter to the lowercase letter with the same name.

A B C D E F G H I J K L M N O P Q R S T U V W X Y Z
a b c d e f g h i j k l m n o p q r s t u v w x y z

Example:

① T — t, w

② Y — y, w

③ U — u, n

④ W — w, m

⑤ Z — z, x

The Names of the Letters | Letters "Ss" to "Zz"

Matching Upper and Lowercase Letters

Directions: Draw a line from the uppercase letter in the left column to the matching lowercase letter in the right column.

A B C D E F G H I J K L M N O P Q R S T U V W X Y Z
a b c d e f g h i j k l m n o p q r s t u v w x y z

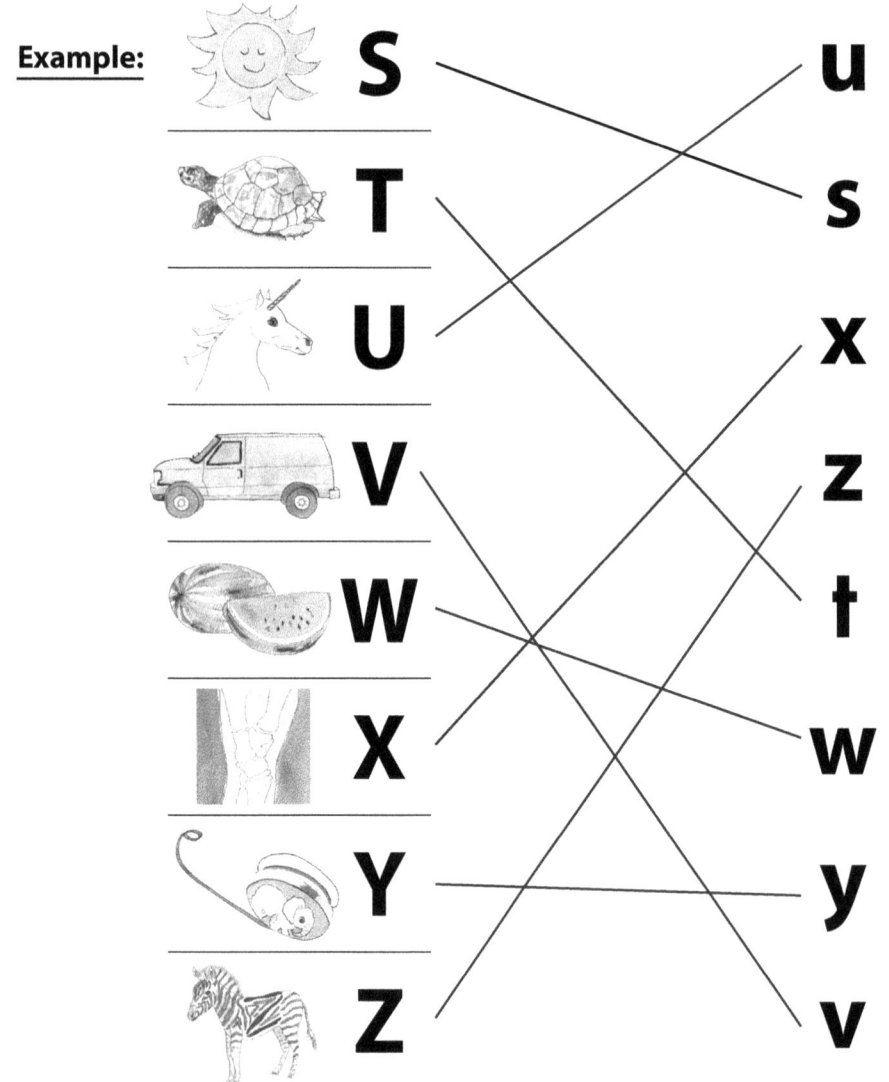

Example:

S

T

U

V

W

X

Y

Z

u

s

x

z

t

w

y

v

The Names of the Letters | Letters "Ss" to "Zz"

Matching Upper and Lowercase Letters

Directions: Cut and paste the lowercase letters next to the correct capital letters.

A B C D E F G H I J K L M N O P Q R S T U V W X Y Z
a b c d e f g h i j k l m n o p q r s t u v w x y z

Example:

S `s`

T `t`

U `u`

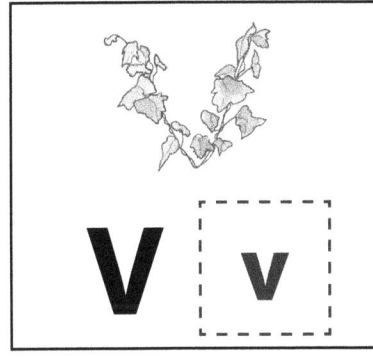

V `v`

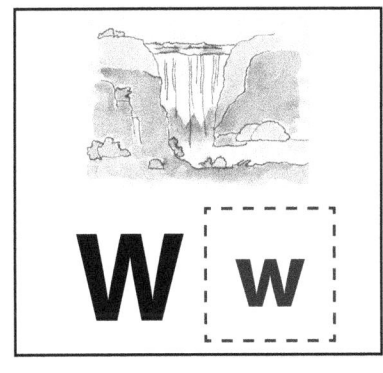

W `w`

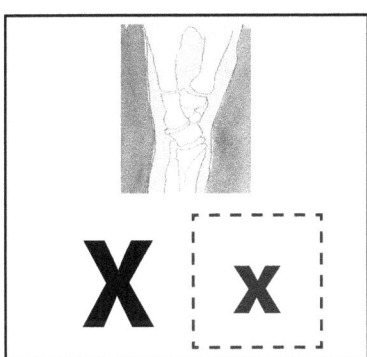

X `x`

Y `y`

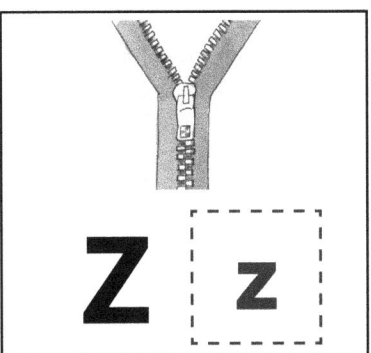

Z `z`

w t z x s v y u

Learning to Read
Letter Names and Sounds

Lesson 4

STARTUP
LEARNING

The recorded teaching sessions
for this lesson can be accessed
at LearnToReadOnline.org.

A. Color the Vowels and Consonants

Directions:

1) Color the vowels red. Color the consonants green.

A B C D **E** F G H **I** J K L M N **O** P Q R S T **U** V W X Y Z
a b c d **e** f g h **i** j k l m n **o** p q r s t **u** v w x y z

Examples:

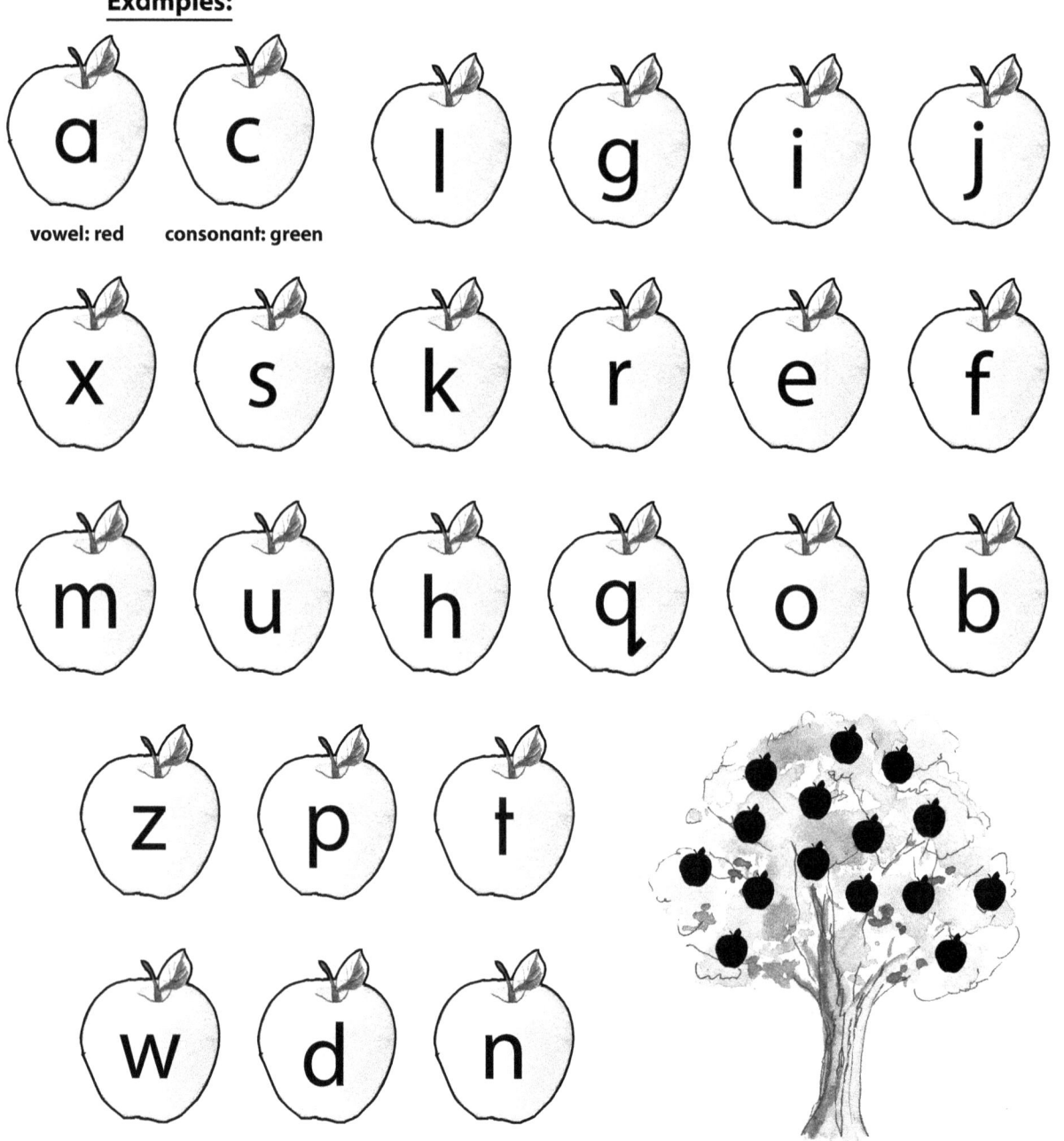

vowel: red   consonant: green

B. The Sounds of the Letters

CCSS.ELA-LITERACY.RF.K.3.A

Beginning Sounds

Directions: Circle the letter that makes the beginning SOUND for each drawing.

Example:

1 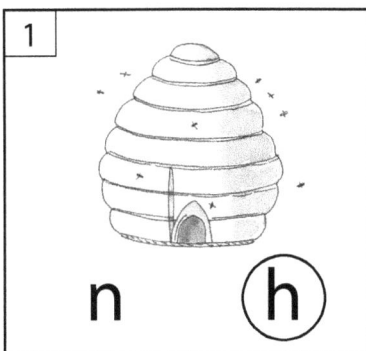 n (h)	2  (d) h	3  (k) h
4 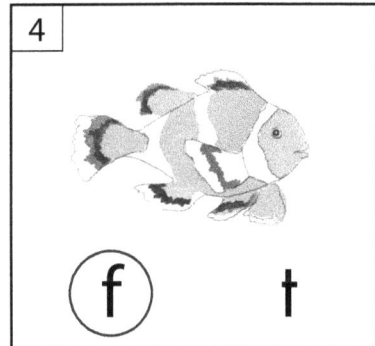 (f) t	5 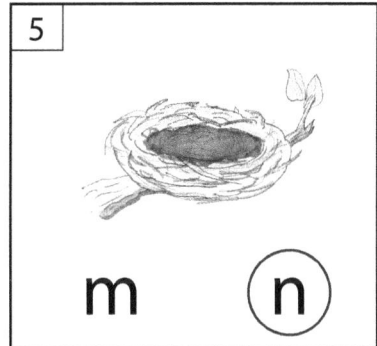 m (n)	6  t (b)
7  h (g)	8  (c) n	9 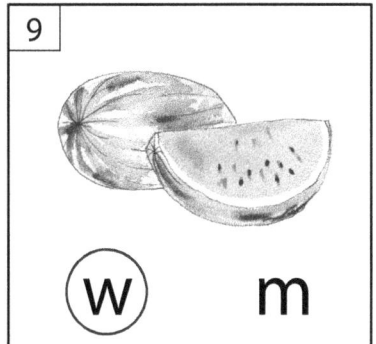 (w) m

1. hive 2. dog 3. king 4. fish 5. nest 6. bear 7. gate 8. castle 9. watermelon

B. The Sounds of the Letters   CCSS.ELA-LITERACY.RF.K.3.A

Ending Sounds
Super Challenge!

Directions: Circle the letter that makes the **ending** SOUND for each drawing.

Example:

1  **(g)** f	2 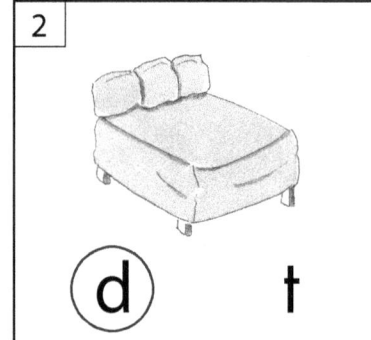 **(d)** t	3 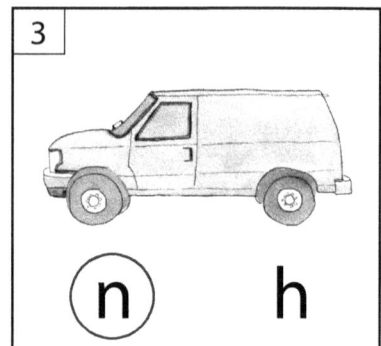 **(n)** h
4 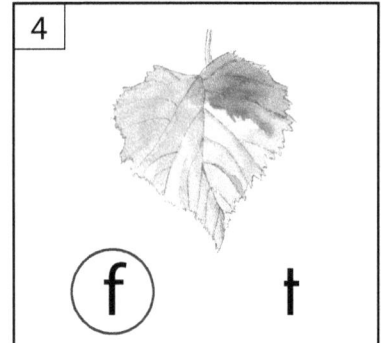 **(f)** t	5 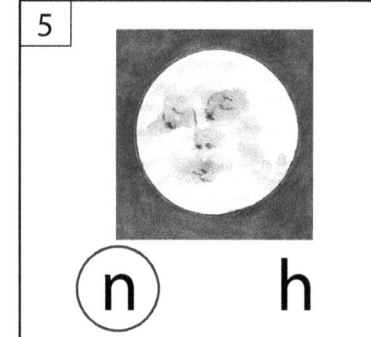 **(n)** h	6 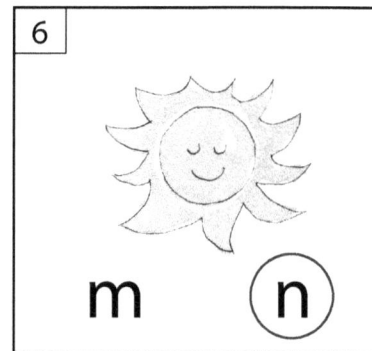 m **(n)**
7 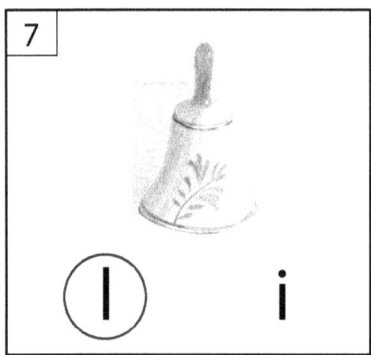 **(l)** i	8 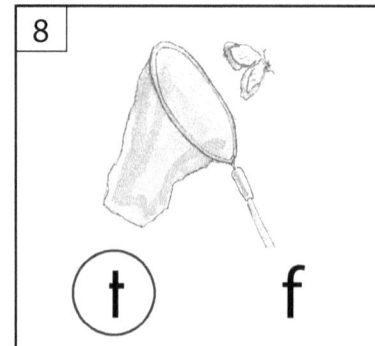 **(t)** f	9 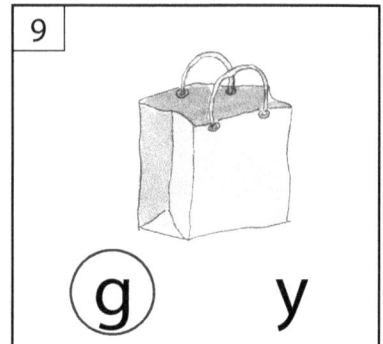 **(g)** y

1. dog 2. bed 3. van 4. leaf 5. moon 6. sun 7. bell 8. net 9. bag

C. Color the Upper and Lowercase Letters

CCSS.ELA-LITERACY.RF.K.3.C

Directions: Color in the picture by matching the upper/lowercase letter sets to the color in the key.

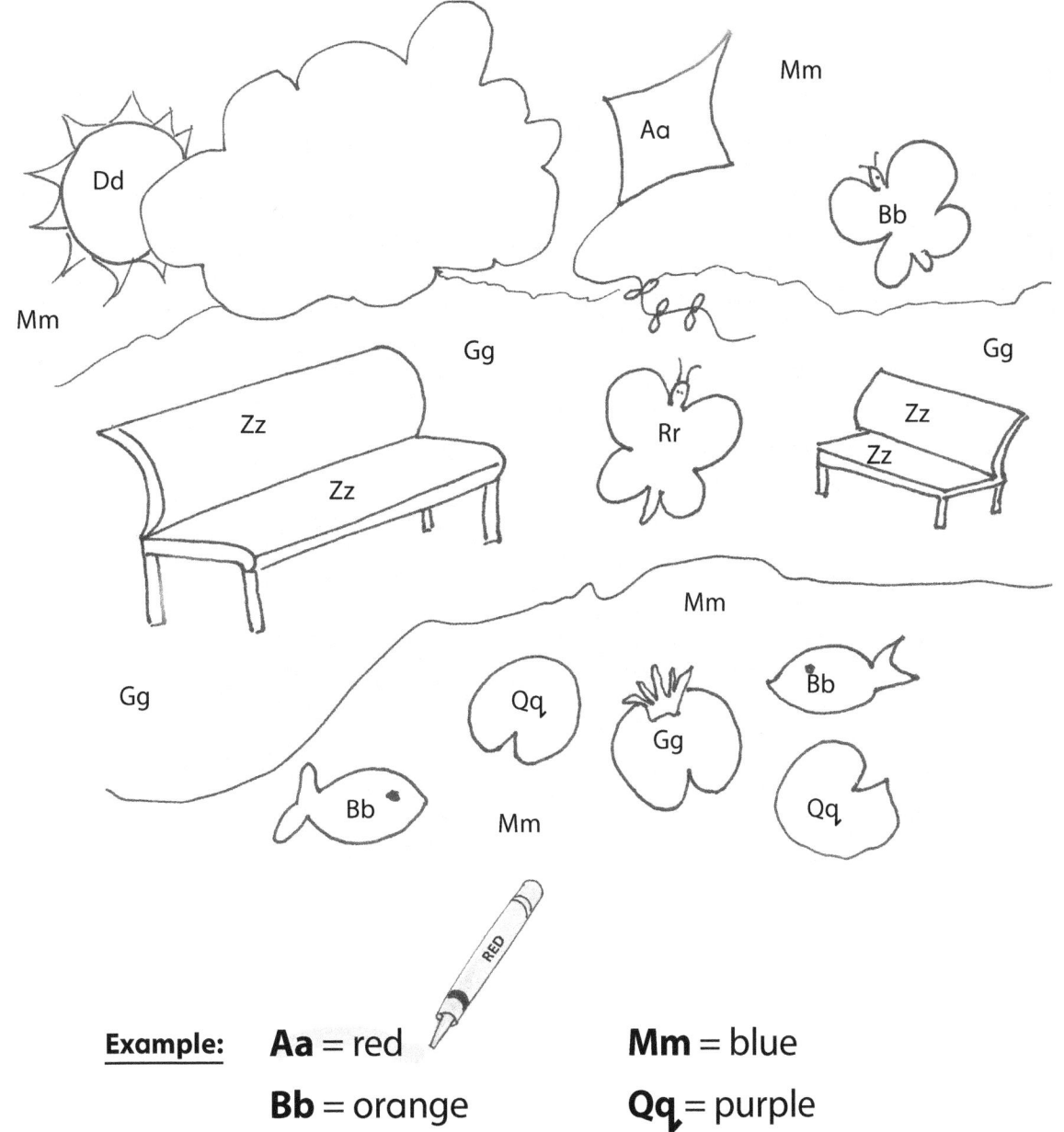

Example:

Aa = red

Bb = orange

Dd = yellow

Gg = green

Mm = blue

Qq = purple

Rr = pink

Zz = brown

Congratulations

You have completed Startup Reading

Learn to Read
Letter Names and Sounds

_____

Student Name

_____

Teacher Name

STARTUP
LEARNING